Bulletproof Your Farm!

Warning!

There are three things a farmer would never do:

1. Graffiti their shop door.
2. Burn money out of their wallets.
3. Admit to faults.

This book will take you less than an hour to read, and within a week you'll do all of the above actions because you'll see things from a different perspective.

Don't read this book until you are ready for real changes on your farm.

You've been warned.

Bulletproof Your Farm!

Andy "Caygeon" Junkin

Independently published

Bulletproof Your Farm! iv

To buy copies of this book online, go to: www.amazon.com or www.stubborn.farm

To buy books in bulk, please call 800-474-2057 or email caygeon@stubborn.farm

To sign-up for our free Masterclass or attend one of our game-changing workshops visit: www.stubborn.farm

2nd Edition: Copyright © 2022 by Stubborn.Farm LLC

ISBN: 9781700393159

Warning: Burning money is illegal. Concepts outlined are figurative. Don't try at home.

ALL RIGHTS RESERVED. No part of this book may be reproduced or transmitted in any form by any means, electronic or mechanical, including photocopying and recording, or by an information storage and retrieval system, except as may be expressly permitted in writing from the publisher.

Published in the USA.

Dedication

This book is dedicated to all farm families who want to keep their family's name on their farm's mailbox for another 50 years.

Bulletproof Your Farm!

Table of Contents

Introduction 3
Chapter 1: ....
Graffiti the Shop Door 15
Chapter 2: ....
Burn Money 41
Chapter 3: ....
Admit to Faults 55
Chapter 1: Part B ....
And Everyone Happy..................... 77
Conclusion 87
Appendix 103
About the Author 119

Anything you can do to improve the quality of your decision-making systems helps eliminate the frustrations of working with family and improves farm profit exponentially!

Introduction

Being Right

When a farmer throws a rope over a barn beam and climbs that beam to hang himself, that is a definite decision. The farmer is saying to the world, "There isn't another way to fix this problem." We all know that isn't true. There is always another option.

We haven't talked about what led to such a definite decision. Absolutely, mental health and farm economics could be contributing factors, but what is the actual root cause? Think about this...

Prior to that moment on the farm, there was a decade of bad decisions on the farm, where partners didn't listen to each other. A climate where partners wouldn't consider other options, and the solution had to be their idea or they weren't interested. It was more important for them to be right than for things to be right, and as a result everything went wrong. They were stubborn. A series of damaging decisions led to a definite decision with long-term consequences.

Now, it's highly unlikely you've ever considered suicide, and I'm pretty hopeful that you have never entertained the idea (if you need help for thoughts like these, please get the help![1]). But there is no doubt that if you are farming with partners, you've gotten into fights where things got out of control and it became more important to be right. This is wrong and is killing us on so many levels!

Farming Has Changed

We've all recognized that farming has changed dramatically, due to advances in technology such as tractors, genetics, and computers.

One of the biggest changes in farming that isn't often considered is that back in the 1960s when Dad was 60, he'd retire. Now, Dad is getting hip surgery and farming into his 90s. The health sciences are a game changer, and this is fantastic!

What I want to highlight is the profound impact that this change in health sciences has had on the culture of agriculture. With farmers living longer, we suddenly have two, three, or four generations farming together. Instead of there being one boss on the farm, you have many bosses! With the economies of scale required to farm, it only makes sense for everyone to stick together, including siblings and cousins. Instead of one dictator on the farm, you have many dictators! Everyone is stubborn. This is leading to everyone butting heads and pulling the farm in different directions. This stubborn power struggle is leading to bad decisions or decisions not being made at all. This dysfunctional decision-making has led to dysfunctional businesses and dysfunctional families. It's killing us!

Crisis Then and Crisis Now

We continuously compare the '80s farm crisis to the economic situation we are heading into right now, but we need to acknowledge the elephant in the room. Think about the following.

In the '80s, when a farmer got bad news from the bank, they'd have no one to talk to. Farms were mostly sole proprietorships, right? The farmer relied on their own decision-making skills (hopefully running to their spouse for advice once in a while). But after getting bad news they'd go out and plough, think through the situation, head into town on a rainy afternoon, make some big decisions with key people, and (hopefully) save the farm. It was that uncomplicated to make decisions.

On most family farms today, you've got three or four business partners who, because of how dysfunctional the family is, can't make simple decisions to change farm production, let alone make complex decisions like changing the business model. Decision-making has become so much more complex compared to the '80s!

Within the dynamics of a multiple-partner business environment, we get stuck on being right instead of things being right. Going back to that farmer who throws a rope over a barn beam: People talk about mental health and what goes on in the mind 10 seconds prior to a farm suicide. No one talks about the decade of everyone butting heads and insisting on being right. I assume your farm isn't that extreme, but there is money slipping between the cracks, relationships that have you walking on eggshells, and frustrations that are never talked about until someone blows up in anger. All of this because some families can't make decisions together.

Nobody has a crystal ball to the economic future of farming. In 2022 when this book is being updated, commodity prices have shot up but so have input prices and interest rates. After COVID nobody really has any sense of certainty with what the future of agriculture holds. I think we need to hope for the best but prepare for the worst. Instead of waiting until you're behind the eight ball, I think it's better that you are proactive as a family and do everything you can do to improve farm efficiencies together as a family PROACTIVELY.

Our next farm crisis isn't going to be due to drought, high interest rates, or a war in Europe. It's going to be due to multiple partners being stubborn, unable to make decisions together to react to the times.

The Good News

What if this potential crisis catalyzed your top competitive advantage? During the '80s farm crisis, farmers hoped to heaven that they had made the right decisions and saved the farm. They really had no one to back up their decisions except themselves.

- What if you simplified the complexity of decision-making with multiple partners?

- What if you turned working with family from a weakness into a core strength?
- What if you turned multiple partners into an indestructible, bulletproofed team that could take on the world together?

In the next few chapters, I am going to show you how you can turn working with family into your top competitive advantage by implementing three simple ideas. But even more importantly, these three simple ideas will eliminate a lot of the frustrations of working with family. Farming with family can be fun again!

Bulletproof Your Farm

People argue that today it's the economies of scale that's the determining factor of which farm will succeed, and which will fail.

First, it doesn't matter how big of a farm you have; you always make excuses about how you could be more efficient if you were bigger. It's not the cards you are dealt but how you play them.

If compare a farm that is worth $40 million in assets with a farm that's worth $5 million in assets, there may be things that make the bigger farm less successful. On that $40 million farm, the family doesn't talk to each other at all. They are constantly butting heads and pulling the farm in different directions.

It's the same butting heads culture of the $5 million farm, they recognize they won't be farming in five years, so they decide to change things fast. On that farm, the family evolves, radically improving how they make decisions together and working toward the same goals. They retrofit how they work together so that instead of bickering, they work as a real team.

I ask you:

- Who is going to be farming in a decade?
- Whose farm do you want to work on daily?
- Whose holidays do you want to be at?

In *less than an hour*, you'll learn how to stop being tough on one another and help motivate your family to make tough decisions as a team so that you can bulletproof your farm against anything.

Overall, my goal is to help you evolve your farm's business culture so you can make the right decisions that will bulletproof your farm against any tough times—now and in the future. My hope is that the processes outlined in this book will give your farm a *competitive edge* so that your family will still farming in 2040 and beyond!

Chapter 1:
Graffiti the Shop Door

Feeding the World

The Chinese have a billion people to feed and are now determined to do whatever it takes to feed their people cheaply. They've had food shortages in the past and won't go through one again. Using a right-wing puppet government, in the next five years Chinese money will burn and clear land in Brazilian rainforest equivalent to all productive agriculture land in the US Midwest. All this land will put double the amount of corn and beans onto the world market. Cheap food is their goal.

Our politicians can't keep consistent policies from one news cycle to the next, while the Chinese think in terms of 10- and 50-year strategies. They have a 70-year track record of making 10-year plans and executing them. They don't mess around! When they plan to have cheap food within 10 years, you can believe they'll do it.

The implications of technology on commodity prices are even farther reaching. Mark Cuban, one of the investors on TV's *Shark Tank*, put our times into a simple yet profound perspective. He said that between 1950 and 1980 there were quite a few patents filed, but there were no serious changes in how society functioned over that thirty-year period. From 1980 to 1995, there was the invention of the home computer, and in that fifteen-year period the white-collar world changed fundamentally. Finally, from 1995 to 2003, there was the internet revolution, and in that seven-year period, everything changed.

Each period of advancement was cut in half, and the changes were more advanced. Think about how smartphones have changed society in just three years.

Farmers tend to be latecomers to technology. Computers didn't change farming in the '80s in the same way they changed Wall Street. Yet the technologies that are now coming down the pipeline are game-changing!

Just look at what happened with GMO corn: yields have gone up and prices tanked. Wall Street has poured billions into developing technologies that are about to change our farms in ways we haven't yet comprehended.

What Are We Doing?

For the past hundred years, farming has been a game of keeping up with the Joneses. We compare ourselves to our neighbors and compete. We do this in all aspects of life, from buying equipment to taking happy family photos.

We compete financially, too. As long as you are better than the other guy, the banker is going to foreclose on them, not you. As one banker said, in order to be a successful farmer, you need to be in the top 50%. Each time there is trouble, the bottom 10% fail.

Being just as good as everyone else, that is, average, may have worked before, but it isn't the way it works now. We are in a different era of agriculture and we haven't fully realize the implications. We aren't competing with neighbors, we are competing with someone producing the same commodity at a cheaper cost on the other side of the world. Now, banks fear folding because over 50% of their clients are verging on bankruptcy.

Growing up on a farm in Bobcaygeon, Ontario, I remember going over our farm's financials with my father. We had all the papers spread across a ping-pong table, and I said, "Dad, this isn't good. We need to make some changes."

Dad said, "Well, I did just as good as everyone else." I couldn't argue with that, because it was true. I came from a very backwards, hillbilly region, where, in the '90s, some families (like my Uncle Murray) were trying to eke out a living with 30 beef cows. The world economy changed and pushed our entire region out of production. We never changed, and we lost the farm.

The question is, if you believe you've got to rapidly change your farm to survive, how do you motivate your partners to make those changes?

This was my struggle on my own family's farm and a struggle that every farm family will encounter. I finally discovered the answer after rewinding my story and putting it on pause for almost 10 years.

A Farm Boy from Bobcaygeon

The day I left for agriculture college my mother showed me our farm's financials. We hadn't made money in over five years. She said to me, "If you don't fix these numbers, I'm leaving your father." Now, it is my job to motivate farmers, but with a line like that, she's better than any motivational speaker!

I went to agriculture college hellbent on saving the family farm. I did an independent, one-on-one course with a university professor where I wrote a 200-page plan on how to turn around the farm. My dad glanced at the cover, opened the firebox, and threw it straight in the fire.

I wrote 18 business plans by my graduating year. I filled five plastic totes of photocopied research backing up my assumptions. Nothing got read. When I came home to farm, my dad's abrasiveness turned nasty when he ploughed my crops under in the middle of the season. For years I wondered why would a man be so resistant to change when he was about to lose the farm and his family? Then I realized the answer.

When young lads come home from agriculture college, they have 1,001 ideas to improve the operation. The first couple ideas Mom and Dad try to go along with, even if some of them are just plain stupid. After a while, suggestions for change feel like criticisms of what Mom and Dad have done in the past. They have worked their entire lives to give the farm to the kids on a silver platter, and the kids are looking a gift horse in the mouth and trampling on the gift. Believing that kids as disrespectful, Mom and Dad shut down every suggestion for change, whether it's good or bad. The kids bite back and reject Mom and Dad's suggestions. You can guess where this goes—nowhere good. Each generation, each partner is constantly fighting for control, never listening to each other. Pride takes priority.

My family were beef farmers. Back in the '70s, things were profitable (or at least we broke even). But then, many people became vegetarians or started eating chicken, and beef consumption dropped. We entered a new price level.

For a five-year average, we were getting paid $0.83/lb., while according to our county extension agent, our COP was $1.20/lb.

My mom said our accountant got frustrated with my father and told him that he had to do something different or lose the farm. Dad chose to call him a paper pusher and ignored him.

I remember going to protest rallies and throwing eggs at politicians, thinking it was their fault that we were in such a mess. A politician told my dad that "the nation needs farmers." He promised a big government bailout. It delivered only pennies on the dollars we had lost. This false hope hurt us.

My dad chose to believe only economists who predicted wildly optimistic rises in prices. I remember my parents arguing and

Dad saying, "The markets will go up anytime now." I'm sure that hasn't been said in the Midwest by any farmers this past year...

I thought the solution was to increase beef consumption. In my teenage years, I went door to door, like a Jehovah's Witness, trying to convert all the vegetarians in my hometown to beef. For me to try to convert the 13 vegetarians in Bobcaygeon to eating beef was a drop in the bucket compared to what we needed.

The truth was that we were in a new price cycle, where demand for our commodity product had dropped. The truth was that our COP was 25% higher than what we were getting paid. We needed to somehow change our production practices so that our COP was less than what we were getting paid.

Why vs. What

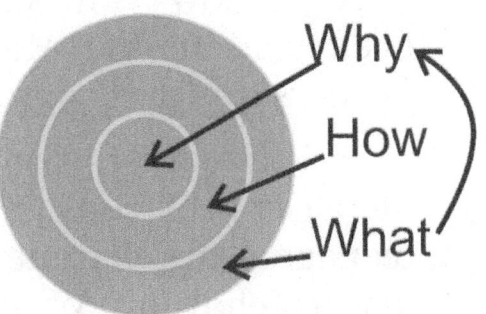

It took years but after analyzing what I had done, I finally realized the mistake I made. I was obsessed with *what* I wanted to tell my dad. I shouldn't have focused on suggesting changing to no-till or intensive grazing. I should have first focused on *why* I wanted to make changes. Dad, mom, and I needed to first agree on a common goal that we could work toward together.

Dad took each suggestion for change as a criticism of what he had done in the past. He didn't see the need for change and thought the markets would change instead. My dad's identity was being a good farmer, and each suggestion for change was an attack on who he was as a person. He felt that it was the government's fault he was failing, not his business model.

Instead of talking about buying a combine or changing the rate of fertility, I first needed to get my parents unified on a common indisputable goal of increasing the COP above $0.83. Instead of my father hoping the markets would go up (what I call top-line thinking), I needed to shift Dad's mindset to bottom-line thinking. That would have made the farm bulletproof at the lowest price the markets could go. If we could survive the worst-case scenario, we could thrive in any other situation. We needed to work toward a common why.

Driving Aimlessly

Imagine a father, son, and daughter team embarking on a road trip in an old, beat-up truck. The son wants to go skiing in Utah; the father wants to enjoy the sun in Florida; and the daughter wants to go to the South By Southwest concert in Texas. The daughter hangs concert passes from the rearview mirror, the son throws skis in the back of the truck, and Dad comes running out of the barn in a speedo and flip-flops. They all look at each other funny but not a word is said because, of course, everyone wants to go where each partner wants to go, right? No questions, right? They just pile in, crank the music, and head out on their journey.

The father starts driving south while his kids nap. Then the son takes over and steers off toward the west. The daughter drives southwest into the night. And still not a word is said.

At the end of the week, they won't admit to being lost, but they are out of money, out of gas, and stuck in a snowstorm in Muskogee, Oklahoma—definitely not a place worth singing about!

The moral? If a family doesn't take the time to talk about—and agree on—a precise end destination, its members will always end up miserable, in a spot where no one wants to be.

Had the father, son, and daughter just talked it out, they could have compromised on a place they would all have liked: Nashville, for instance. They all could have had a good time there doing different things. They could have been there in 10 hours instead of spending a frustrating week going nowhere.

This is how it is with a lot of family farms. We have power struggles within our families that cause us to farm in ways where no one is happy. How many farms do you see where one partner pushes for high milk production and another partner pushes for lower cost? Every day they are arguing because they aren't shooting for the same goals. On most family farms, miscommunication and egos impact the farm's bottom line more than the markets and weather together. We are driving around aimlessly and getting nowhere fast.

What you need is agreement on a destination. I used to be a big advocate for business plans, but I no longer think this is as important as having a simplified goal. When you plug a destination into a GPS, you can still stray off course, but as long as there is a destination, you can get back on course. If everyone agrees on the end point, then like a GPS, everyone can recalculate the route together figuring out how to get there.

BHAG

In 1961, President John F. Kennedy said, "We are going to put a man on the moon in 10 years' time." It seemed like an impossible goal, since half the technology needed didn't even exist! But even after JFK was assassinated, the goal was still achieved. Why? Because the goal was so simple and profound that it inspired an entire nation. Thousands of scientists overcame their larger-than-life egos and genius quirks to work as a team to do the impossible. This was arguably the greatest BHAG (big, hairy, audacious goal) ever.

Since then, what has NASA done? Nothing even close to that significant. The reason? Their mission statement is multiple paragraphs and just way too complex. It's not one line that everyone can remember. Without the simplicity of one line, NASA has been working toward a mess of different goals, accomplishing little.

You need a BHAG that is so simple you could spray-paint it on your shop door!

BHAG is a term Jim Collins came up with in his book *Built to Last: Successful Habits of Visionary Companies*. Roughly defined, it's a phrase you'd put on a t-shirt and remember two weeks later. Google's BHAG was "Organize the world's information." Microsoft's BHAG was "A computer on every desk and in every home." The concepts were so simple that thousands worked toward the same simple goal. Many companies tried to do the same thing but failed because they didn't have all of their employees focused on what matters. One simple line changed everything for those companies!

Every farm is going to have a different BHAG.

Niche Marketing

Trying to be the lowest cost producer isn't for everyone, and I have farmers who do the exact opposite. After losing his shirt in the commodity markets, one farmer bred his Angus cattle with Wagyu cattle in order to create a tastier beef. His goal was to sell it to the white tablecloth restaurants. Yet nobody was driving 300 miles to buy beef from the freezer in his garage, and he was selling overfed steers at auction for pennies. It wasn't until his family set the BHAG of selling "100% of 100 steers/year at $10/lb." that his family's marketing mindset shifted. To do this, they realized they had to put effort into marketing the less-desirable cuts of beef at a premium, not just the strip loins. Today, they are selling over 80% of their steers at $10. This BHAG turned around a nearly bankrupt farm to the point that they burnt their mortgage and their son now farms with his family.

Grandpa's Rifle

As part of my process when working with farm families, I establish a central goal that everyone works toward and every partner can remember off the tip of their tongue. One farm came up with "30/30 & everyone happy."

It's short and memorable. They set a goal of getting input costs in the bottom 30% of the state average, yields 30% higher than the mediocre neighbor they combined for, and everyone going home happy every day. They had this mission statement burnt into the stock of Grandpa's 30/30 rifle, which hung above the shop door. They went from going home ticked off every day to actually getting along within weeks. Their profitability spiked because "30/30" was "sticky."

Settle Arguments

When your BHAG is sticky, it is more likely you can remember it even amid an argument.

In 2013, two brothers got into a financial mess. When corn was $7, they were losing $200 an acre! I got them to set a target and spray-paint "$3" on the side of their shed. Later that month, they got into an argument and one brother grabbed the other brother by the shirt and was pulling his arm back to punch him when his sister-in-law yelled across the shop, "What does this have to do with $3 corn?"

That moment forever changed the farm. They realized that infighting and crying over spilled milk wouldn't get them anywhere. Within three years, they were producing corn at $3.10 a bushel. It worked; they dropped their COP by half. You can apply the same philosophy to make it work for you!

I am a big believer that every farm family should spray-paint their BHAG on their shop door in the ugliest spray paint they can find. And when I mean ugly, the uglier the better!

That is because every time you open the shop door, it should tick you off! If you have a fancy BHAG written on a sheet of paper sitting in a filing cabinet or even framed, you'll forget it. But if it's on the shop door, you'll see it a dozen times in a day. More importantly, your uncle Billy who never reads anything but is a genius with a welder will see it a dozen times a day, too. He will be equally ticked off about having ugly spray paint on the shop door but will at the same time be thinking about ways to actually achieve the goal and realize that if it doesn't happen, you won't be farming in 2030. Getting everyone focused on the same goal is key!

Herding Cats

Recently a 10,000-acre farm that had four cousins farming together lost their bank financing. Everyone thought of them as one of the best farms in Kansas and when the local banker threatened to pull their financing, they thought the banker was just giving them the gears. Losing their financing hit them like a frying pan!

Within nine days I got them replacement financing, but the bigger thing was that I got them to agree to a common business strategy, which included the BHAG "10%." It meant:

- Dropping their input costs by 10%
- Reducing their cost of living by 10%
- Having 10% of land contracted to a niche crop (Aramanth) that will get them over three times more income per acre
- Laying off nonfamily employees and everyone giving 110% effort
- Aggressively marketing beef and selling 10% of steers online that year at $6/lb.
- Selling 10% of their land and equipment

Ten months later, they had achieved all of the above goals and the farm was in a better strategic spot than it had ever been. On the day we started, this was seen as impossible!

Their 87-year-old grandfather had asked to stay out of the strategic planning process because he needed to reduce stress for his heart condition.

However, when he had seen that I had convinced his grandsons to spray-paint their BHAG on the shop door, he was livid. I contended: "If you don't have that goal on the door, they'll forget what we discussed today by next Tuesday. Now, they'll think about it every time they go past it. If they achieve the goal, you can always afford to buy a new door, but if they don't you won't own the door in two years." Grandpa just grunted as grandpas do.

Six months later he told me, "You know that painting-the-door thing? I thought you were crazy, but it worked! Getting the boys to agree on anything was like herding cats. Spray-painting the shop door turned the farm around!"

Chapter 2:
Burn Money

How do you turn around a farm?

Yes, getting a BHAG in place is key, but what will get your partners back on course when the daily grind gets in the way? How do you hold yourself and your partners accountable to get sh*t done?

You burn money, of course.

Let's say that every week at the same time and place your family sits down for a 30-minute family meeting. At this meeting each partner has to come to the table with one simple idea on how to improve farm profit by at least $3,000 without spending more than a $1,000. The rule of thumb is that for each dollar spent, you've got to get at least three times as much back, and it's preferential that you don't spend anything, focusing on little management changes.

For instance, on a dairy farm you could look at how to reduce your farm's somatic cell count or increase your pregnancy rate. If you're a cash cropper, you could figure out how to reduce the number of days it takes to plant corn, gaining a bushel per acre each day.

If you come to a meeting without a valid idea, you are forced to pull $10 out of your wallet, put that $10 into an ash tray in the center of the kitchen table, and burn your money.

Take a $10 bill out of your wallet right now and stare at it. Imagine if I tried to force you to burn that $10. How would you feel if you burnt $10? Would you do it repeatedly without changing behavior?

The fear of having to burn another $10 next week, at the same time and place, will stimulate you to think of new ideas.

Why should your family force you to burn that $10 for not coming to the table with an idea on how to improve farm profit? Because there are hundred-dollar bills laying around every farm—little tweaks that, if made, could result in thousand-dollar improvements.

But I'm Perfect

You might think that you are the epitome of good farm management and that there is no way anyone could squeeze an extra nickel out of your farm. You have the best farm ever.

Yet have you even tried to identify problems or missed opportunities with your partners? The dysfunctional family politics that exists, to some extent, on every farm prevents family members from taking the initiative to explain ideas for improving efficiencies. We overlook these problems or sweep the mistakes under the carpet instead of ruffling feathers.

Now imagine, at the same time on the same day next week, you are sitting down with your family, and you have a group pact that if you don't have a good idea to improve farm profit, you'll have to burn another $10.

I guarantee that you'll think of an idea on Sunday night while you're showering or on Tuesday afternoon when you're ploughing. You'll write it down on a scrap piece of paper. Then you'll spend an hour on Google researching the idea, and you'll come to the next meeting with the idea researched.

What will be the result?

You'll come to the table with an idea on how to improve farm profit. Everyone will spend roughly an hour prior to next week's meeting to do the research on how to squeeze out an extra thousand dollars.

It won't be a half-baked idea, because if you don't come to the table prepared, *you have to burn $10*. Everyone holds each other to the same standard and the hour is very productive.

You think you don't have time to do homework? How much are you losing on your farm because nobody forces you to sit down and research? What is more important, forking sh*t for an hour or fixing $1,000 mistakes?

How much frustration do you have with your partners when they just put one foot in front of the other and aren't critically thinking about ways to squeeze thousands out of the farm?

I strongly believe that farming is a lifestyle, but if we don't treat it like a business it won't be a good lifestyle. Read that sentence again. There has got to be a time and place to treat farming like a business and squeeze extra profit so everyone's long-term lifestyle goals can be achieved.

If you improve farm profit by at least $1,000 a week per partner for the next five years, you'll be able to achieve both your business and lifestyle goals.

Why do I know you'll do that? Your fear of burning money is a catalyst to creativity.

Listening

But when you pitch your ideas, your partners will never listen, will they? Previously, probably not. But not now.

Why? First of all, you never had a time and place to discuss ideas in a constructive manner. In the past, ideas were thrown out when your family was trying to not get into a fight or when your partners had other concerns they were thinking about.

Second, if your partners don't feel a partner is giving proper courtesy or listening to another partner's ideas, the group can vote for the discourteous partner to burn $10. You don't have to agree with another person's ideas, but you do have to be open-minded and listen.

One of three things will come of this:

- Your family decides against the idea. Through the process of throwing the idea around, you

or one of your partners sees a flaw in the concept.
- Your family tables the decision pending more research or a better time for it. Not everything is a priority. You schedule a discussion for a later date.
- Your family decides to go with the idea, or a version thereof after group collaboration. It results in real changes happening on your farm.

When you build a fire, you start with kindling and then add bigger logs when the fire can handle it. It's the same way with farm decision-making. You should start with making small $1,000 decisions together first and then expand the scope of decision-making later.

Evolved Decision-Making

I once had a family with $17,000,000 of debt sit down with the need to cut (or squeeze out extra) $3,000,000 within months in order to survive. It would have made sense to talk about selling land or increasing milk production. Yet the conversation quickly turned into an argument between households about whether dog food was a personal or business expense. One family lived on the farm with a dog and the other family lived five miles down the road. One partner walked out crying and no changes got accomplished that day.

Too often families who are constantly bickering over small or silly decisions try to tackle complex strategic planning (ex. succession planning), and it blows up in their face, because they stink at making decisions together.

I always suggest for a family struggling with serious farm debt or farm succession issues to spend three to six months problem-solving small issues like $1,000 production improvements before taking on complex, $100,000 decisions.

Likewise, a family that gets along fabulously now can take their decision-making from good to great on simple $1,000 production improvements. They'll be able to discuss complex issues at a sophisticated level after a little practice.

Accountability

Once the family makes a decision, it's a done deal, right? Wrong!

This is where burning money is critical.

One of agriculture's biggest problems isn't the swine flu or aphids, it's follow-through. We are plain lousy at implementation.

On even the most successful farms, I have found that over half of all strategic decisions fail to be implemented because farmers get distracted by day-to-day activities. We get sucked into fighting fires instead of preventing them. This burns us!

After each meeting it is critical to write down:

- What decisions were made
- Who is going to do what and by when

Start each family meeting by looking at the calendar and reviewing the tasks that were supposed to be done by that date.

If something wasn't done by the due date, it doesn't matter why, that person has to burn $10.

This process creates an intense level of accountability within your family that instills zero tolerance for failure.

It humbles everyone and eliminates egos. Dad is no longer "better" than his children; he is a partner. Outside of the meeting, the family patriarch or matriarch can still be the boss, but in the meeting everyone is equal. No one can provide excuses. It's a time and place to talk about business and evolve family relations.

Burning money creates a new mindset everyone on the farm lives by:

"Say what you'll do, and do what you say."

Chapter 3:
Admit to Faults

When dealing with generational conflicts, I've noticed that the apple doesn't fall far from the tree. Whatever bad habit a parent might accuse their kid of having, the parent frequently shares. Often in family disputes, the pot calls the kettle black. For instance, I've seen sons accuse their fathers of having a short temper when they share the same bad habit to some extent.

Looking from the outside in, it can be funny to watch. Often what irritates you most about a family member is a trait you're guilty of. You might not display that trait as profoundly as a relative, but it's there to some extent. You only have to think about the neighbors to laugh at this irony.

When I start working with a family, the first thing I get them to do is to adapt something I call The Farm's 10 Commandments.

Similar to the 10 commandments Moses brought to his people, such as "Thou shalt not kill," I get the family to adopt rules on how to work together that everyone on the farm can buy into. I get the farm to identify:

- **Five good values or habits** that everyone agrees has made their farming partnership successful to date but that the family struggles to implement now. (ex., work ethic)
- **Five bad habits** that everyone agrees are the farm's weaknesses that make it difficult to work on the farm and the family wants or needs to turn into strengths. (ex., temper)

If you can get everyone abiding by these easy-to-recall values, then the next time your partner and you get into a heated debate in the shop, the matter can be decided based on these values.

Values We Need to Continue

Several years ago, a small chicken hatchery called me up. The son had just graduated from college and had come home to join the family business. Part of the reason this hatchery was successful was that the founder worked alongside his employees and did the dirtiest jobs himself. Yet his son was the last one to work and first one to leave; he was afraid to get dirty.

After a few months, the dad started to step out of the hatchery and left the son to manage a crew of nine men. These employees were some of the toughest men in the county, many of them having prison records. They showed the son no respect, and one day, the son got set up in a physical altercation with an employee. Simply put, the employees had no use for "the frat boy," whereas they had infinite respect for the founder. This is because the founder had earned the employee's respect, whereas the son felt entitled to it.

After this altercation, we broke down why the son was having problems managing the men. The phrase "you've got to earn your respect daily" came from this discussion, and it was added to the farm's 10 commandments. This one line changed everything within that operation. The son learned to "earn everyone's respect daily," ranging from his father who loved him to the employees who despised him. The son started becoming the first one to show up to work and the last to leave. He worked alongside the men (whom he previously "supervised" while playing on his cell phone) and did the toughest jobs. The rate of employee turnover and absenteeism increased dramatically. Dad stepped out of the hatchery altogether, letting his son take over management.

One line changed the son's attitude. It's the line he repeats to himself when he reacts to the alarm in the morning. It is what causes him to go to bed early instead of drinking with his high school buddies on weeknights. It changed who he was. He now represents everything you'd want in a successor. That hatchery has grown from hatching 2.5 million chicks to 12 million birds in less than a decade partially because of this one phrase.

Values We Need to Change

On one farm, there was Grandpa, who was old school and didn't understand why talking about the culture on his farm was so important, until the week after the first meeting.

The following Tuesday, Grandpa sat on the tailgate with a mason jar of nails. After breakfast, he had six hired men pulling apart an old shed. With each board, they had to pull the nails out and straighten them. Grandpa dropped each nail into the mason jar.

The grandson had just come from picking up supplies in town and was disturbed to see Grandpa making the men pull nails out of boards. Even though this was how Grandpa was able to build this farm from nothing, times were different now and a new mindset had to be adopted. The grandson said, "Grandpa, we've got to stop pinching pennies and start focusing on the dollars. It's great that we saved $5 in nails, but we just spent $75 in labor."

Grandpa was about to get bitter and drive off, but then a lightbulb went on, and he gave this big smirk. The week before, the family had written "stop pinching pennies and focus on the dollars" as part of their 10 commandments. A few words got them on the same page in their approach to management. Instead of Grandpa driving off mad, this adaptation of common management philosophies eliminated half the fights on that farm.

It's Not Rocket Science

As a mediator, I have witnessed how opening up about each other's pet peeves can turn ugly pretty quickly. Families will start throwing stones at each other for bad habits they themselves are guilty of, and it just turns into a cat fight.

What your family needs to do to work around this tendency to throw stones is to collectively identify bad habits or traits that everyone could improve upon as a group. I used to spend hours talking to farm families about developing 10 commandments unique to their farm. Although it's true that every family is unique and will have unique problems, most neighbors share similar faults. It is perhaps a relief to know that you aren't the only family with these problems behind the barn. What I've found is that a family can go through a list of fifty common values (see the appendix for a list) and within minutes "cherry pick" ten resolutions that fit them almost to a T. Obviously, if everyone makes improvements in turning their weaknesses into strengths, the farm is going to be a much better work environment within a year.

I'd encourage your entire family to read this book and look at the appendix, where I list fifty common business values that are often weaknesses on family farms. Why not have your family go through this list and pick out 10 of them that you all identify with. If your family adopts these commandments and each individual works hard to fix their bad habits, within three months, you'll have a completely different business environment.

Through the completion of this exercise, everyone will have developed internal discipline and resolve and will be 10 times more apt to fix problems that are unique to your farm.

Accountability Is Everything

By the family collectively adopting resolutions for change, everyone can be held accountable to the same standards. For instance, if the family identifies temper as a bad habit, everyone can hold each other accountable to keeping their cool as a resolution. When (not if) a family member loses their temper, someone else can call them on it by saying "That's $10 you owe at our next meeting" and walking away. At the next meeting, the family can hold the guilty partner accountable to paying the $10 fine. The fear of having to burn money in future meetings will gradually reduce the frequency of temper tantrums.

The most important part of burning $10 is the resulting open discussions about the root issues, which lead to real change. It isn't just a matter of discussing what was going on in the mind of the hot head but also of examining what problems might have led to the incident, including things like buttons others pushed to get the person so agitated. For every incident, the family has to put together an action plan of changes that everyone works on to ensure a similar incident doesn't happen again. For instance, one partner might have to make a change (ex. not be late for work) to reduce the stress that caused another partner to lose their temper. Going forward, they will be held accountable (ex. pay $10 fines every time they are late to work), which will resolve within three months the root issues that cause HR problems on your farm.

If you can get your family to identify a handful of bad habits that everyone needs to change to some extent and motivate them to make the changes, you'll be amazed by the results.

Three things I've noticed:

- Instead of giving a partner the cold shoulder for their behavior, there is a time and place to call a partner on their shortcomings. This allows everyone to focus on their partner's positives the rest of the week, creating a happier workplace. Dislike the sin, not the sinner.
- By holding everyone accountable to the same standard using monetary fines, power struggles will be eliminated and standards will increase. The dynamics of family and business won't get mixed up. Where respect is an issue, this process is amazing at

rebuilding partner relations fast!
- For farms where parents are reluctant to transfer assets because they aren't confident in the next generation's capabilities, it will either become evident that the kid isn't serious about farming or they will change their bad habits.

When a family collectively changes 10 bad habits, they create a mindset where everyone is open to admitting mistakes. Then fixing production or financial problems will be 10 times easier. It will be like pushing water downhill instead of up!

And now for something completely out in left field...

What About Bob?

I spoke to Bob the night before we sat down with his family. The farm had forecast a $200,000 loss for the next year, and Bob was discouraged, believing that the farm could lose money for a longer period of time than they had equity to borrow against. Bob was concerned that he was going to have to sell the cows and retire rather than set up his daughter, Sue, with the farm.

I sat down with Bob and Sue the next day and got the family to brainstorm ways to improve farm profit without spending more than a $1,000. We flew in a management consultant who had turned around large herd dairy operations across the country for over 30 years. We included the farm's vet and nutritionist in the meeting. Within three hours, we had seven solid ideas that could result in $500,000 in reduced costs and $200,000 in improved profit by increasing the milk yields. This was a $5 million dairy, and in the course of three hours, we figured out a way to improve the dairy's profit by 10%.

You would think that Bob would be ecstatic that in an afternoon, without any significant investment, the farm went from having to pull the plug to turning a profit. But he was furious. That is because several of the areas suggested were areas of his responsibility. He felt criticized.

For instance, Bob was responsible for feeding calves on a daily basis. The vet suggested the farm sell the bull calves at five days of age instead of 30 months, because they were losing over $500 a head on feed costs and could profit $100 a head if they sold them earlier. The farm was amazing at milking cows yet lost money at raising calves because their rate of gain was lousy. Raising calves was one of Bob's responsibilities, and his son had been suggesting the same idea for years.

Bob took great pride in his management skills and saw the discussion between the vet, the accountant, and Sue as a raving criticism of Bob's past management decisions. In the meeting, he agreed to make the changes, but one by one, he nixed each idea over six weeks, becoming resistant to any suggestions for further change. In the end, Sue quit in frustration, and Bob had to sell the farm. Today nobody is happy.

Why did Bob fail?

If you want to turn around a family farm within six months, it's not done by looking at the farm's financials first. It's done by the farmers themselves changing internally.

What do a farm's 10 commandments have to do with a guy like Bob, who won't change?

Twelve years ago, when I started mediating, everyone expected me to come onto their farm like Judge Judy. They would sit around the table shifting blame onto everyone else. It always turned into a catfight. Within minutes, nobody cared about finding a solution, everyone was concerned about personal survival and self-esteem, and crazy stuff happened fast! This is why so many mediations fail.

You might have heard of this guy called Jesus. I'd like to think he's a really good friend of mine. He was once quoted as saying:

You hypocrite! First remove the beam from your own eye, and then you can see clearly to remove the speck from your brother's eye. Matthew 7:5

Regardless of whether you are a church deacon or an atheist, these words can truly transform any farm. If you can get each partner to acknowledge that 5% of their character or behavior has to change, you can transform any farm's business culture overnight.

Before you sit down to turn around a farm, you don't first go over the farm's financials, you get everyone to change a few bad habits.

How do you take a guy like Bob who is stuck in his ways and won't admit to needing to make any changes? You first get him to admit to needing to make *a* change. Any change. Then you talk about making production changes.

If you have a farm environment where everyone is defensive and shifts blame, you'll get nowhere fast. But if you have a business culture where everyone is committed to evolving themselves, where everyone becomes all they can be, by working on themselves, you can radically transform any farm. Start with inward change, and outward changes will happen more easily and quickly.

Google this: Self-Actualization "What a man can be, he must be."

Chapter 1: Part B
And Everyone Happy...

In chapter one we talked about the importance of setting a specific financial goal for the farm in the form of a BHAG. We talked about the importance of spray-painting one number on the farm's shop door (graffiti the shop door).

This is important to do. However, I strongly believe you should write down that number (whatever you decide upon) and write "and everyone happy" right after it.

Too often when creating business goals, we lose sight of what is important. For instance, I had a farm that grew from selling 3,000 acres to 20,000 acres of dehy alfalfa. The son Carl was sleeping only a few hours per day in the shop while running the dehy plant overnight, and in one three-week run he didn't once get home to see his wife and kids, who lived seven miles away. He had three kids under the age of seven. The patriarch acted surprised when he found out his daughter-in-law wanted a divorce. The family had a successful business, but it came at the expense of Carl's marriage.

The root issue this family had was that they focused on growing a successful business but didn't focus on what it would take to grow a successful family. There wasn't a common goal of work/life balance.

In general North American society, we have over 50% divorce rate, but in small businesses in New York it's over 80% due to the stress of the business and in-laws have on a couple's marriage. Farming has traditionally had a lower divorce rate than the average due to rural cultural norms; but now that divorce is becoming more accepted in rural communities, the divorce rate is skyrocketing. The possibility of divorce threatens every farm's insolvency. More farms will go bankrupt within the next 10 years than the last one hundred because of this. It is an unspoken epidemic.

I firmly believe that a young farmer has to work more hours (3,000+ a year) than their parents did in order to have the competitive edge to succeed in business. Equally, they have to invest more hours into having a successful marriage than Grandpa and Grandma did.

Entitlement is the #1 mental barrier we have in farming. We all know of neighbors who stop combining early because they think that the work can always get done tomorrow. We also know of neighbors who take their spouses for granted and don't try to nurture the relationship daily. We've seen fathers who never play toy tractors in the sandbox with their kids and cry "nobody is interested in the farm" 20 years later. These are examples of entitlement. You and your partners have to assume you are underdogs, working hard at nurturing both business and family relationships.

But how do you balance work with family life? Whether you are a farmer or software entrepreneur, hard work is the key to long-term success, yet family life is equally important. The challenge of work/life balance isn't unique to farming. It's a challenge every business owner faces, especially during a business's busy season. Whether you are the CEO of a software company at Christmas time or the owner of a lawn and garden store on Memorial Day or a farmer taking crop off before the next big rain, everyone faces struggles with balance.

The problem is that farmers aren't investing their time like it's money. We treat time as if it's an infinite resource, when in reality it's the most limited resource known to humanity. Time management isn't in our vocabulary.

Arnold Schwarzenegger once said you've got to sleep six hours ad that leaves you 18 hours in a day. You show me how you spend those 18 hours; I'll show you what your life will look like in 18 years. Whether you are a governor, body builder, actor, or farmer, the rules are the same. We are all constrained by 24 hours in a day.

What is the sense in a farmer spending 18 hours a day to grow a successful farm if he doesn't also grow a successful family or find happiness? Why be miserable? You've got to really think through how you invest 10, 14, 18, or 20 hours a day into the business and equally invest your free time on the things you prioritize most in life.

Gone are the days of coming into the house and vegetating on the couch, only speaking to your family to tell them to get out of the way of the television. You've got to work more hours on the business and invest what little time you have with your family wisely, as if spending coin.

Yet how you spend your time isn't solely your decision: you've got to have a consensus with your partners. You can't leave work early if your partner spends three hours longer; that is a recipe for an unfair partnership. Just as it's critical to discuss a financial goal, it's key for your family to discuss personal goals. Just as it is important to talk about budgeting finances to grow successful businesses, you've got to talk about how you are going to invest personal time to grow successful families. Then you've got to hold each other accountable.

If you want to get away from the farm on Saturday afternoon to attend a wedding or go to your sister-in-law's birthday, you've got to discuss that with your partners on Monday. Not the Monday after in anger, the Monday before as a professional! This is so you aren't stuck pulling a calf on Saturday afternoon while your partner is cultivating or watching football on TV. You've got to find out from them what is important to them and how you can help enhance their lives. Planning and budgeting your time as a team can help everyone achieve happiness.

Also making quasi–New Year's resolutions is key. For instance, I had one family set resolutions just prior to planting, resolving what they wanted to do more of during the forthcoming summer.

The son wanted to spend two hours each day actively playing with his four kids, who were under 10. His wife kept a stopwatch on the time that he actually spent playing with them. It was an eye opener as to how little he did get time initially to play with them. His wife and kids forced him to burn $10 for a few weeks, but he grew his bond with his one girl substantially that summer.

Equally his father resolved to go motorcycling four days per month. During the spring, he had to burn $10 a few times, but by the end of the summer he had gotten out on the road almost weekly. That October, he learned he had terminal cancer and thanked me on his deathbed for forcing him to have had an epic summer.

At the end of each day, ask yourself whether you went home happy. If not, why?

Write down anything that went wrong that day and why it went wrong. Ask yourself how you could prevent the problem from occurring again. Think through a solution rather than just griping. Write it down instead of stewing and forgetting. At your next meeting, bring up one of these problems. Similar to how you brainstorm $1,000 improvements, each week your family should brainstorm one idea on improving how you work together. Then as a family, brainstorm solutions to the frustrations you have working together. If your family is able to iron out two to three little frustrations weekly and a few big problems each month, you'll be amazed at how much happier you'll be in a year!

Conclusion

True Ownership

Two pickup trucks met at sunset on a dirt road, mirrors nearly clipping. The father and son hadn't spoken since the meeting with the bank earlier that afternoon. They had applied for a loan to buy the farm next door and thought they were in good financial standing. It shocked them to find out that, in the application process, the bank had identified a major accounting error that jeopardized all their farm loans. The banker said, "You've got 365 days to turn things around, or I'm foreclosing."

The son rolled down the window to his air-conditioned truck. The father already had his '84 Chevy window open and ordered his one son to "give me your hand." The son reached out his hand and the father dropped a shotgun shell into his palm. "I almost used that on myself

20 minutes ago," the father said. "You boys got us into this mess, you boys have to get us out." With that, he tore off, spraying gravel everywhere.

The father was the boss. He had gone into the John Deere dealership the previous August and bought a combine, without discussing it with his wife or sons. He drove it home, jokingly saying to his wife, "Happy anniversary, dear!" He was equally guilty of causing the farm's mess. Yet he blamed everyone else and suddenly played the victim.

I don't have a problem with a man thinking about suicide when he's told that he's about to lose his farm. It isn't right, but it's a knee-jerk reaction and common sense is often overridden by these dark thoughts. It happens more often than we openly admit.

However, I do have a problem with a family patriarch not showing leadership in the farm's moment of crisis. I have a big problem with any leader shifting blame onto others, especially when they were equally involved in causing the problem. Yet this is the way most farmers react!

Just as it's foolish to commit suicide, it's equally foolish to shift blame onto your family and your partners and believe yourself to be blameless. Ownership is more than having your name on a deed in the farm's safe. True ownership is taking responsibility for problems and dealing with them while you still can.

Yet on most farms I walk onto, there is denial and shifting of blame.

If you want to survive, you've got to quickly go from a mindset of butting heads to one of pulling together. This starts by everyone admitting to their contribution to the farm's lack of success and a willingness to change.

It's the polar opposite to the knee-jerk reaction you see with most mediation or farm debt turnarounds. Instead of having an environment of blame and shame, everyone has to be willing to rapidly self-improve.

Every Farm

Every farm has problems. Many farms these days struggle with either farm debt or farm succession issues, and most family farms struggle with how their family works together. Regardless, we don't want to admit to these issues to ourselves, let alone to the neighbors. Expecting your family to not have problems is just as foolish as Ford expecting the Model T to be perfect. You've got to be proactive and realistic about expecting problems.

You won't ever have the perfect farm. Get over that idea. It's that idea that creates imperfections that fester and never get solved. But if you get precise in setting a goal of what you want and get a process of continuous improvement, you'll get closer and closer to your ideal goal every day.

When problems do come up (and they will come up, let's keep it real), you'll have a better framework to solve problems rationally instead of having a power struggle, which leads to failure. If your family problem solves how you problem-solve (using a continuous improvement *process*), you won't have any big problems fester long term!

> **Succession Side note:**
>
> **Until your family can squeeze out an extra 10% profit within 10 months as a team, your family is not ready to discuss where the farm is going to be in 10 years' time!**

Continuous Improvement

By the 1930s, Henry Ford had a line of people down the street wanting to work for him. He had a revolving door for employees, because his policy was "hire the best, fire the rest." If someone didn't meet his standard of excellence, they were chopped off the assembly line. While Ford Motor Company maintained that high standard for decades afterward, by the late 1970s, the company was having serious issues with quality workmanship. Its vehicles were breaking down in the parking lot. Ford was acquiring the reputation of "Fix Or Repair Daily," and Ford couldn't figure out why.

It took Ford nearly a decade and 3 billion in losses until they finally took action. The company looked to an Iowa farm boy named W. Edwards Deming. He was a nerdy guy with graduate degrees in mathematics and physics. He had funny ideas about a concept called "Continuous Improvement"

In the 60's, this American had to go work in Japan because for years no American would take his ideas seriously. Although the Japanese didn't have many competitive advantages compared to the American automotive sector, by the late 1970's Toyota was leaving their competition in the dust, including Ford. This is because the Japanese had listened to Deming's ideas while no one else did. As Japan's reputation for quality and economic power skyrocketed, Ford reconsidered the ideas professed by the Iowa farm kid and wanted to get in on the magic. Ford hired Deming to figure out who was to blame for all the breakdowns with the vehicles.

The problems stemmed from the fact that over 1,000 people were touching each car as it went down the assembly line. Over the course of each car, at least one person was bound to make a mistake. "That was just statistics," said Deming.

But no one owned up to making mistakes, because they didn't want to get fired. The employees were very good at shifting blame and sweeping the mistakes under the floor mat. As a result of this culture, the company was hammering out faulty vehicles.

The executives at Ford were shocked when Deming said, "There is no one to blame, except the executive." He told Ford that management actions were responsible for 85% of all problems in developing better cars. Deming's logic was that, statistically speaking, the probability of there being no mistakes is zero. Statistically, you are always going to make mistakes. The answer was to minimize the mistakes rather than be unrealistic about wanting to eliminate all of them. Instead of expecting there to never be a problem, you should excel at problem-solving by minimizing the number of reoccurring mistakes. In order to do this, they had to address how they problem-solved. They had to change their business culture.

Although we don't realize this, we have the same culture in agriculture. We pretend to be perfect and don't admit to failure for fear of being found at fault. We sweep our mistakes under the carpet and never admit our faults to our partners. We try to pretend we are perfect, and as a result many imperfections are created. We turn a blind eye to mistakes our partners make in a passive-aggressive manner until one day we blow up and show rage as if we were firing someone.

Ford applied Deming's philosophies and it resurrected the company to remain competitive on the world market. Yet most of the American automotive sector didn't and the ideas of this Iowa farm boy almost put the American automotive industry under! Remember how Obama had to bail out GM in 2008?

All I have done was taken the ideas from Iowa farm boy and I am now applying them to American farms in a way that fits the unique parameters of the farming culture.

You can pretend to be perfect and reject change until it is [almost] too late. Or you can embrace your failures proactively, get better at problem-solving together as a family, and have a competitive edge over your neighbors.

What I am suggesting to you is this:

1. **Graffiti**: Set a vision for what success is both for your farm and your personal life. Clearly define where your family wants to be in as few words as possible.
2. **Burn money:** Establish a time and place that you meet once a week to:
   - Squeeze out an extra $1,000 per partner per week in efficiencies.
   - Improve how you work together as a team.
   - Hold each other accountable to following through on promises.
3. **Admit you're wrong**: Get real about the flaws in your business culture that you need to turn into strengths. Everyone needs to evolve. If everyone does this, your farm will be a fundamentally different place within six months.

These steps won't fix all of your problems overnight. But they will fix the fundamental problems of how you can problem-solve and will gradually reduce the problems on your farm. It will give your farm a competitive edge.

True Family Farm

Many people these days complain that the family farm is all but dead. Yet there has never been a generation where the term "family farm" is more relevant. Although more farming assets are under ownership of partnerships or corporations, the vast majority of the shareholders of these entities are relatives. Instead of one person owning everything, a farmer has to share assets with relatives in order to have the economies of scale to farm.

Sharing ownership of assets on paper is easy. It's tougher to share ownership of:

- A dream and have everyone equally committed to achieving it
- Problems and the ability to solve them as a team
- Everyone's contributions to the farm's problems and their need to change

Yet if you can get everyone to share ownership of these things, your farm can gain a competitive edge at no cost!

Talk is cheap. Why not make a commitment to change? Why not fill out the Bulletproof Farm Plan found in the appendix over the next 30 minutes with your partners (who have also read this book), get everyone to sign the resolutions contract on page 118, and then go spray-paint the shop door tonight?

If you aren't committed to making a simple change like spray-painting a BHAG on your shop's door, what changes will actually happen within six months?

You can always buy a new shop door with newfound profits if you hit that BHAG, but if you don't you might not own that shop door in a decade!

Appendix

Bulletproof Farm Plan

1. Set a BHAG.

What is the main commodity that you produce?
(ex., milk)

What is your current cost of production (COP)?
(ex., $16.10/cwt)

What is the lowest price this commodity has hit over the past decade?
(ex., $13.25/cwt)

What is the lowest price you foresee this commodity hitting within five years?
(ex., $13/cwt)

Is "and everyone happy" a suitable goal for your farm?
(ex., Yes)

Thus, what is your BHAG?
(ex., produce milk @ $13/cwt & everyone happy)

2. What are your ideas?

What ideas do you have to improve farm profit by $3,000 by spending $1,000?

1._____

2._____

3._____

4._____

Ex., It takes us too many days to plant corn.

Solution: We need to have machines "field ready" by Feb. 15 and have maps/instructions so employees take less time to manage in May.

What are pet peeves that could improve how you work together as a team?

1._____

2._____

3._____

4._____

Ex., Partner is always showing up 15 minutes late.

Solution: Text 15 min. prior if you are going to be late.

3. What are your commandments?

What are five values that has made your farm successful that your family should resurrect as a core value?

1._____

2._____

3._____

4._____

5._____

Ex., If a successor is lazy when Grandpa clearly wasn't, put "working dawn to dusk" as a value.

What are five values that your farm should adopt to go from good to great and to make the farm more successful going forward?

1._____

2._____

3._____

4._____

5._____

Ex. "Don't lose your cool." Everyone commits to not losing their temper by taking an anger course online.

50 "Ten Commandments" Ideas

Stumped? Here is a short alphabetical list of business values (with sticky sayings). Choose the ones that may have made your farm successful to date that you need to keep or values that you need to adapt to go from good to great...

1. **Accountability-**Always follow thru & own up to your mistakes.

"Say what you'll do, and then do what you say."

2. **Action-**Unafraid to make the big decisions and work hard to execute ideas into reality.

"Well done, is better than well said."

3. **Ambition-**He/she knows what they want and are willing to do whatever it takes to get it.

"The desire not to be anything is the desire not to be."

4. **Assertive-**Address issues upfront vs. passive-aggressiveness and avoiding

confrontation creating a big fight later.

"The cowardly lion was passive aggressive."

5. **Balance**-Able to dedicate enough time for the farm's success and family's success throughout the year.

"Grow a successful business and family."

6. **Communication**-Ability and willingness to articulate thoughts in a way that people want to listen to you.

"The art of conversation lies in listening."

7. **Congeniality**-Works hard daily to make farming fun and make others feel positive about themselves.

"Courtesy is the shortest distance between two people."

8. **Consideration-**Treats everyone with respect, even if they don't do the same to you.

"Do unto others, as you would have them do unto you...not as they do unto you."

9. **Continuous Improvement-** Always aware that there is room for improvement.

"To improve is to change; to be perfect is to change often."

10. **Courage-**Not being afraid to face inevitable problems.

"Courage is being scared to death, but saddling up anyways." John Wayne

11. **Dedication-**Daily giving a 110% to the farm.

"It is easier to do a job right than to explain why you didn't."

12. **Discipline-**Ability to control one's feelings and overcome one's weaknesses.

"If we don't discipline ourselves, the world will do it for us."

13. **Efficiency**-Using time wisely.

"Method will teach you to win time."

14. **Empathy**-Understanding and accommodating other's feelings.

"If you want understanding, try giving some."

15. **Example**-Being a good example of character to partners.

"Example is contagious behavior."

16. **Equality**-Nobody feels the need to be in control of every situation and leadership is based on who is most skilled in the situation.

"No one is the other man's slave."

17. **Forgiveness**-Accepting and giving of forgiveness and pardon.

"We don't cry over spilled milk."

18. **Friendship**-Sustain partners through difficult periods. Day-to-day being fun to work with.

"Treat your friends like family because they are."

19. **Grateful**-No attitude of entitlement and you don't take anything for granted.

"Gratitude turns what we have into enough."

20. **Grooming**-Passing knowledge to the next generation.

"We teach everyone everything we know when they are ready for it."

21. **Honesty**-Being able to admit weakness so that one can self-improve or the team can deal with problems.

"No legacy is so rich as honesty."

22. **Humility**-Not flaunting ones talents and gifts.

"When a man realizes his littleness, his greatness can appear."

23. **Integrity**-Holding true to one's values.

"Integrity has no need of rules."

24. **Knowledge-**Investing time to read farm magazines, attend training seminars and learn new skills.

"Always learning."

25. **Leadership-**Taking control without being controlling.

"Good leaders demand without being demanding."

26. **Motivation-**We motivate ourselves and our partners.

"Don't just motivate, be your partner's motivation."

27. **Objectivity-**Being able to look at a situation from a purely logical position.

"Be objective not objecting."

28. **Optimism-**Being optimistic even when one doesn't feel it.

"When God gives you lemons, make lemonade."

29. **Options**- Instead of arguing about who is right, listen to partners' ideas and problem-solve as a team.

"Many ways to skin a cat."

30. **Ownership**-Taking responsibility for things that are hard to admit to rather than passing blame.

"When you point a finger, four are pointing back at you."

31. **Not Passive-Aggressive**- Address issues upfront vs. avoiding confrontation creating a big fight later.

"Head in sand creates a sandcastle out of a mole hill."

32. **Patience-**Capacity to tolerate delay, trouble or suffering without getting angry or upset.

"Patience isn't about waiting, but having a good attitude while waiting."

33. **Perseverance**-Willing to do whatever it takes to succeed. Doesn't give up when the going gets tough.

"The gem cannot be polished without friction, nor man perfected without trials."

34. **Perspective**-Willing to see things another way.

"People aren't influenced by things, but by their thoughts about things."

35. **Positivity**-Nobody habitually "drops" negative or divisive comments in a way that poisons the workplace.

"No poisoning the water bowl."

36. **Problem-Solving**-We solve problems as a team.

"Identify your problems but give your power and energy to solutions."

37. **Professionalism**-Courteous, punctual, and dependable.

"Professionals do their best even when they don't feel like it."

38. **Resourceful-**Being creative and innovative.

"1+1=4"

39. **Respect-** Shows the proper respect to family and employees every day.

"Only those who respect the personality of others can be real use to them."

40. **Responsibility-**Having internally driven sense of duty to deal with problems and get results.

"Accepting that you are the cause and solution to the matters at hand."

41. **Sacrifice-**Willingness to put the farm or family needs before your own.

"The farm comes first. Always."

42. **Self Awareness-**Aware of ourselves and how people see us.

"To know oneself, one should assert oneself."

43. **Service-**We work on the farm but we serve our family.

"Service is what life is about."

44. **Success-**Everyone has a clear shared understanding of what success looks like and what they have to do to make this happen.

"The best place to succeed is where you are with what you have."

45. **Teamwork-**Believes in making decisions together and working as a team to solve problems.

"Definition of business is mutual helpfulness."

46. **Thrift-** Able to live and farm within your means.

"Thrift is poetic because it is creative; waste is unpoetic because it is waste."

47. **Transparency**-The right hand knows what the left hand is doing at all times, and why they are doing it.

"Lack of transparency breeds distrust."

48. **Tolerance**-Ability to tolerate the existence of opinions or behavior that one does not agree with.

"The words of the close-minded fall on deaf ears."

49. **Victimless**-Instead of working yourself to the bone and complaining about it, get better at communicating with partners about sharing workload and delegating tasks.

"No more 'woe as me' mentality."

50. **Work Ethic**-Having the consistent drive daily to work harder than anyone to achieve your dreams.

"We work to become, not to acquire."

Resolutions Contract

Our partners have all read *Bulletproof Your Farm* and agree to try to implement the book's principles over 13 meetings. Over the next 12 weeks, we will meet every week on _____ (day) of week at _____ (time).

For each meeting:

1. I will have a credible idea that costs no more than $1,000 but gives three times the Return on Investment.
2. I will listen to everyone's ideas with an open mind. I will not force my opinion but work with partners to make joint decisions.
3. I will have tasks done on time, as promised from previous meeting.
4. I will burn $10 as a form of punishment if I fail in any of the above resolutions.

We will meet on __/__/__ (13th meeting) for a strategic planning meeting. At this quarterly meeting we will focus on solving $50,000 problems and family issues. We will then weigh this program's merits and decide if we will continue this process.

By signing below we agree to these terms:

About the Author

My name is Mark Andrew (Andy) Junkin and I was the seventh generation to farm in Bobcaygeon, Ontario. At college there was no other farm kid as zealous about where he's from—97% of friends still call me "Caygeon." You can too.

In 2003, my dad went to an auction sale and my mother yelled out as he was leaving, "Don't bother buying any more farming equipment until you have a business plan with your son." My dad came home with a manure spreader, and I guess you could say "the fit hit the shan". This triggered their divorce and eventually the end of farming for me. Ever since, I've been turning cr*ppy situations around, starting off by helping my friends and over the past decade across America.

In my travels, I fell in love with a Midwestern farm girl. We now live on a homestead just outside of Mount Vernon, Iowa, with three boys, Huck, Colt, and Scout. They are my hobby!

I'm not a lawyer, accountant, or Dr. Phil. I'm just a farm boy who, since walking away from his family's barn in

2007, has been OBSESSED with figuring out how to **help stubborn farmers work better together**. This has been my only income source since I opened my office in Ontario in 2010, and since marrying Bernadette in 2019, I've been based in Iowa. Initially, my company was called Agriculture Strategy, but we renamed it to Stubborn.Farm to better represent my niche and unique services.

I help farm families stop being stubborn with each other and help each farmer to become stubborn at turning bad habits into good habits to be the partner/friend anyone would want to work with. Family, farm succession, and farm debt issues are easily solved – once you "fix the stubborn."

To be frank with you, when I was farming, I would have told you that my niche of fixing farm family business culture is B.S., but I've gone through a lot of B.S. since then and am hellbent to make sure that your family doesn't go through the hell that mine did.

www.Stubborn.Farm

To sign-up for our online Masterclass or attend one of our game-changing workshops visit: www.stubborn.farm

Last-Page Summary

Farming's #1 mental barrier is entitlement. We inherit farms from our grandparents and just assume we'll gift it to our grandchildren. Just because your family had a successful farm 10 years ago doesn't mean you'll still be farming in 10 years. Being a business owner and living in a nice house in the country is a privilege, not a right!

To ***Bulletproof Your Farm*** you've got to assume that:

The markets aren't going to be ideal.

Your farming practices aren't ideal.

You aren't always ideal to work with.

In order to still be farming in 2040, you've got to assume that you are the underdog! Armed with this mindset and the three tools in this book, your family can implement radical changes that gives you the competitive edge that bulletproofs your farm against anything.

Made in the USA
Monee, IL
27 January 2023